THE
PALACE THAT THE APOSTLE THOMAS BUILT IN INDIA

St. Jacob of Serug

Translated by: D.P. Curtin

Dalcassian
Publishing
Company
PHILADELPHIA, PA

Copyright @ 2010 Dalcassian Publishing Company

All rights reserved. No part of this publication may be reproduced, distributed, or transmitted in any form or by any means, including photocopying, recording, or other electronic or mechanical methods, without the prior written permission of the publisher, except in the case of brief quotations embodied in critical reviews and certain other non-commercial uses permitted by copyright law. For permission request, write to Dalcassian Publishing Company at dalcassianpublishing at gmail.com

ISBN: 979-8-8690-9338-7 (Paperback)

Library of Congress Control Number:
Author: Curtin, D.P. (1985-)

Printed by Ingram Content Group, 1 Ingram Blvd, La Vergne, Tennessee

First printing edition 2010.

THE PALACE THAT THE APOSTLE THOMAS BUILT IN INDIA

Lord, Lord, give me the word filled with light and open my lips in love to proclaim your deed, Son, in whom the human race was buried and raised, awaken my mind from the darkness in which it is enveloped. The evil one threw me down into a grave, into the silence of those who hate me. Through you it (the human race) has been raised up, like Lazarus, from darkness. Anointed stone, which he did not carve with his hands, through you the thing will be strengthened, which I have set up like a building. The sea of the Apostle Thomas is infinite, allow me to steal from him who stole from your side. He stole while being worthy, allow me to steal while being unworthy. Whoever steals from the thief gains wealth. I will give it to your church, do not hinder me, and take it from yours, Lord, I give it to you. Son of God, knock at your door with a pure heart. Open me your treasure, that I may take and give to your household (to the sons of your house). Thomas was traveling with merchants from Mahuzah, seeing how a hunter hunts to gain something. The bridegroom and the bride stayed with him in a demure manner. The apostle went away, and the Lord (Christ) dwelt with them.

The king rose early at daybreak and went in to see them, but he was very astonished that they were together; he even saw the bride with her face uncovered in front of her bridegroom. He became excited about what a new course of action this would be. But the king, being excited, began to say, "What new behavior is this that I see here?" "Has foolishness befallen those who live with us?" It was fitting for them to veil themselves from strangers. Now she sits freely before her bridegroom, and her appearance is cheerful, her heart is joyful, and her face is uncovered. The king called her and asked her: "Why don't you want to veil yourself, especially because of this day? People will say how she violates propriety by uncovering her veil in front of her husband on the first day. Behave modestly, even if your mind is happy and cheerful. Draw the veil over your face before strangers."

The bride replied: "I cannot veil myself; for the veil has been taken away from me and I have seen the light. Another betrothed man came into the bridal chamber and became engaged to me there. But if you knew who the bridegroom would be who has now become engaged to me, you would truly strive to be. How much he has prepared for me with the dowry he promised me. Neither the sea, nor the dry land, nor the whole world, nor the wealth of the kings and princes of the world, nor of the rulers, can outweigh it; indeed, all worlds do not equal his great wealth. That Hebrew is his servant and his disciple. He told me about him, about how rich he is. After his servant (Thomas) left, the king (Christ) himself appeared to me and I have I saw his glory, how splendid it is, and my mind clung to him. I have united myself with him in love in a chaste manner; and I do not consider any creature like him, because I love him; and if I die for him, I am not sad, and if I fall into the fire for him, I am not grieved. Heaven and earth do not cause me to separate from him, because I am united to him in love and hate everything else that happens. And if sword and violent (terrible) death threaten me (or rise before me), I will not forsake the love of him who has betrothed himself to me forever.

THE PALACE THAT THE APOSTLE THOMAS BUILT

The bridegroom said: "And I love him lovingly. Marriage but I despise and hate him because of him. He said to me, He who does not sanctify himself is not worthy of my Christ. I left the bed of sexual intercourse and earned his love. He promised me that for this temporal bridal chamber there would be that bridal chamber whose bliss lasts forever. He takes him up to heaven who believes in him, and in the place of light he (the believer) dwells there without dying. As he told me, his servant (Thomas) built this human dwelling in six days without any artists. But he sent that Hebrew, who came here to India, and as he (Christ) told me, he went here for carpentry. The king wants to build a palace, and he (Christ) sent it to him (the king); because of this matter he is now traveling with Canfians. But as I have heard, he will build it (the palace) up in heaven if the king gives him as much gold as he needs. If you are willing, come and let us build us a palace on high, over which even death cannot rule. In a short time we will build it, although it is great, for he has taught me the art of it.

The King heard these words and tore his clothes; he lifted up his voice and he wept loudly with excitement over the palace which the apostle Thomas built in India. He saw the young people helping each other. His mind became confused, so that he believed it was magic. He heard words of truth from them, and considered those young people to be liars, for the evil one (Satan) had spread the garment of error over his mind, and these words of understanding were not pleasing to him. For his conscience was corrupted by the poison of idolatry. He went away from there like a serpent in great anger against the young dove (Thomas) that had flown away from him into the nest of India. He went away in threat, like Goliath against David (1 Sam. 17:43), going around in the streets looking for Thomas. But the bridegroom and the bride became servants for the King on high. Yet, the wretch did not recognize that he was the one to whom they belonged, and he believed that he was greater than he was. Thomas went with the merchant to the region of India, the grace of the Lord being with him, as with Joseph. The news reached the king of India that Thomas had come down and Chaban, the merchant who bought him, also arrived with him. And the king left everything and immediately asked for the architect. The king sent and called for the merchant as soon as he heard it, so that he could find out from him about the builder whom he had brought, whether he could build a palace as he asked. But Chaban came before the king and greeted him. But he asked him about the builder and about the route.

THE PALACE THAT THE APOSTLE THOMAS BUILT

Chaban replied, "The power of the Lord went before me into Judea, and he showed me how I should walk. I came to a man, the lord of the area (Christ) and greeted him. I revealed the whole matter and told him truthfully. I saw him rise and perceived that he was an upright man. I reported to him and revealed the whole truth to him. I told him that I had come to buy a servant and to bring him to our area to build a palace for the king, which he had seen in a dream. 'Find me a master builder here, if you are able, who is experienced, insightful, wise and skilled in the art of building, who carves stones and builds temples, carves wood and sets doors, makes windows, builds houses, builds a palace, builds rooms and apartments, makes ships with wood and boats, and there is no art of architecture that he does not understand.' Is it possible to build a throne for no reason? Where do you see a house built without stone carving, other than what Thomas built in the middle of India? He will do something in our area that has not yet existed in the world, and will show us something that we have never heard of before. I also told him about your kingdom, how big it is, and I told him that among all the kings there is not one like you. I said that the architect should come down to the King of kings to perform his service, before whose majesty kings and rulers tremble. When I told him intelligently, he opened his mouth and let a voice that aroused confidence sound into my ears. He saw that I was from afar and was anxious for a servant, and I said that I would buy you a servant such as you asked for. But before I spoke, he showed that he knew what I wanted, and like one who knows what is hidden, he revealed everything. I have never seen a man like this among men, nor such love and knowledge as was spread in Ihra. He opened his lips to speak and I was struck with astonishment. The troubles left me through his speech and my mind was attached to him. He revealed to me what was in my heart and what had not been born. He confessed, and what I thought he learned immediately, everything that was in my mind. I will describe that miracle, shocking it, to your highness, without my mouth being enough to speak of the man. Humble and of simple speech, forgiving and peaceful, understanding and insightful, splendid and beautiful, perfect and simple, great and famous. His words are like pearls, and even more than the eyes, they capture the heart to love them. He concluded a purchase contract with me, and shared and weighed the silver which he had determined. He described to me the skill of the servant, which astonished all of my senses. But after he heard that I said how wonderful it was, he told me that it was something to be despised for his art and he told me about the artist (God), from whom he learned, who can build a palace in an

THE PALACE THAT THE APOSTLE THOMAS BUILT

instant. I believed he would demand a thousand pieces of silver from me, but he said to me: 'I demand twenty pieces of silver for him.' I believed that he was mocking me and I spoke again to get it from him to learn the truth, and he repeated the same word to me again, no less, no more. His word was one, true in both yes and no. So I heard him give orders to the servant, whom I took. But I weighed the price and bought the servant using bills of sale. But he confessed (in the purchase letter) that he was selling him and he wrote and gave it to me according to the law. But he even gave back the price of it to the servant when he went away. But I was amazed at why he sold him and gave him his price, so he was worried that the servant might not be lucky enough to overcome me and therefore gave it to him. I noticed how he walked about the palace that the apostle Thomas built in India. He gave him orders and praised him. I was also very surprised that he gave him his award, though I know not why and for what purpose he did this. I believe there is some secret in it and after some time we will probably learn the truth. We can also get to know his (Christ's) works through his (Thomas's) deeds. Command me, Lord, to come to him and learn from him whether my words are true. He is worthy to come and enter and stand before your throne; for he is wise and your crown will not be dishonored by him. He is perfect in insight, prudence, arrangement and in art. However, my praise is not of today, after some time you will be reminded of me by the servant whom I have bought."

The king ordered that Thomas come so that he could learn from him the truth of Chaban's words. He entered, and Chaban with him, as the king had told him. Thomas bowed his head and greeted him according to custom. But Thomas noticed that the king was amazed. Yet, before he spoke, he praised his beauty. He was amazed at his beautiful appearance and his modesty. He resembled an angel in appearance and beauty. But the king looked at Chaban, his face brightened, he smiled and said: "Truly beautiful is the servant whom you have brought with you. However, this appearance is not that of servants and slaves previously bought forth. But I don't know what kind of new thing this is. Did the king cunningly send him as a servant to scout out the area, see the people and then bring an army? Behold, O Chaban, will not the servant whom you bought make us poor, and steal our possessions by cunning? It is probably the case that this servant manages the king's administration, that is, acts as a higher official for him, or he is a general and came to our country because of the war. His master sent him to fight as a servant and took his prize and cunningly issued a bill of sale. The thing is too wonderful, I believe that there is a secret in it. From your story everyone can see how surprising it is. For the price of a servant, you have bought an artist equal to kings, who, if he came just to measure, is worth twice as much."

Thomas replied: "Don't worry about that, Lord! In reality I will build, for I also came to construct. Do not fear because of deceit, which is far from me. Our friend, who used it, was strangled by the rope (Judas Iscariot). For the Lord, who is with me, hates deceit as he hates murder, and he will not allow the deceitful to come near him. That I am an artist, I will immediately prove to the masses, and convince you that there is no fraud in the servant's selling. If you want me to build you a palace, you will find out what kind and how skillful a servant Chaban has bought for you. But I will also reveal to your Highness the matter why the Lord sent me to this land. The gentleman who sold me is a builder and the head of artists, and if I were to describe his art to you, you would not believe it. The artist is admirable, and the ear is too small for his deeds. If someone were to talk about him, it would seem unbelievable to the listeners. He built a structure that no mouth can describe, O Lord. Wonderful deeds he performed, too high and unknowable to register as knowledge. At last it pleased him to build himself a building, which the evil ones destroyed in his envy, but he rebuilt it. In my absence he showed my comrades how he had stood up, and they told me, but I didn't believe them, I thought they were liars. I contradicted them and said: 'I do not believe that the building has risen, I have not seen it, but you are deceiving me.' Then he showed himself to me in reality and I examined his side and looked at his parts, how true! But because I doubted the building, he swore, saying, 'I will sell you as a slave, because you doubted.' This is the circumstance for which I was sold, O Lord King. You now know the whole thing as it happened. I have hope in God that I will build the palace. Rather, everyone should be amazed at the building where it rises. His call will be heard after my passing, even if I have already gone home, and he will remain an eternal memory even if I am already dead. But your rubbish will also become great, O king. Kings tell stories and cities proclaim the news of him to the ends of the earth, the countries and regions, after centuries it is still reported to the news of your glory. Kings desire to dwell in him and they are not admitted, and those who have power over him do not allow themselves to

THE PALACE THAT THE APOSTLE THOMAS BUILT

see him. Whenever you want, we want to go and build, I have nothing against it. We just want to wait for the right day and I'll start."

The King said: "Let us see where it is convenient, let us build it; and where it can be built and what is suitable for it. Take the measuring tube and measure for me how it needs to be built. Determine his walls, divide his windows, define his room; denote there the house of the bakers and the house of the cooks; separate the places for the arts from each other in the royal castle, which will become magnificent through your knowledge."

Thomas replied, "We want to go immediately and look at the place, and it is in your opinion that it should be built. Come, just see by indicating where it should arise. Then command gold to be given and another (Christ) will take care of the construction. I have hope in God that I will build you a palace, whose splendor kings strive for their possessions."

The king said: "Let us go to see your art; and from your measurements I will know, I will see the accuracy of your words. I get to know you from the first measuring rod you put on, and I understand your actions from your measurements."

The king went out, and with him the apostle, carrying the measuring rod, to measure the earth, while the Messiah was building it in heaven above. He measured and made windows for the light and windows for the wind, and also chambers and rooms for the summer and winter, and the house for the bakers according to the sun and he measured out space for water ponds. He designated the apartments for the crafts of the royal palace. For the cloth weavers and gold miners and for the silver workers. Furthermore, he measured and added the house for the ironworkers, the house for the woodworkers, the house for the painters, and the place for the horses and mules. He built the treasury in the middle of the square because of the buildings, and he left a few windows for light and made them small. The king rejoiced greatly, and called Chaban, saying to him: "Truly the man stands tall as the head of an artist, and his insight is rich, and he is great in knowledge, and his understanding is bright. His judgment

THE PALACE THAT THE APOSTLE THOMAS BUILT

inspires confidence. I have never seen such knowledge as this man's among men, and no understanding of the execution of what must be done that equals his. He should begin immediately and take gold as much as he can. I will give him, who is so wise, everything he wants."

The king said: "Indeed you are an artist. Your insight is also worthy of serving kings. Take gold and start, I want to see it soon. Lay the foundation and I will rejoice with you and then depart. My heart has rejoiced and my mind has rejoiced in your measurements. I'll be happy now when I see its basics."

The apostle saw that the matter required alms, and in the king's presence he could not give it unless he departed. Thomas said, therefore: "It is not a suitable time to begin with the building. Give me gold and someone else (Christ) will take care of the building. In Tishri one must begin. We want to build in the winter and rest from work in the summer, for the building that is undertaken in the summer, winter comes, and tests it. And if it is not firm, it will not endure. But anyone who builds his house in winter does not have to worry about winds and storms attacking him from the winter onwards, for after the building has become solid, neither winds, nor storms nor weather. Now let the king build in the winter, as I have explained, for the building will be good. It is to be built and workers will be found, and they also need it. But give gold and go in peace wherever you go. I hope that by the time you return, I will have built it."

The king said: "You understand your skills. Take gold, and when you want, start clearing. Build the palace for me and begin and finish it whenever you want. If you can, encourage him so that in a short time it will stand erect." He ordered Thomas to give gold and left immediately.

The apostle took it and went to the poor, distributing it. He hired workers who immediately built without wages, he gave gold and encouraged them to build saying: "All workers work beforehand and receive then wages, they continue to build as soon as they receive praise and paid for what they ate. But they, because they had received reward beforehand, should not slack off and stop showing even greater effort with the happy ones as true happy people do. The poor fed themselves and put great effort into prayers; but by their prayer they built a palace in heaven and completed it. They prayed on earth and the Messiah built it in heaven above. Building without work, they build like eager, skillful people. The poor took the wages, ate and were satisfied. They were glad and gave thanks. Instead of stones, they built the palace for the king with words. But Thomas sent word to the king so that he would give more gold. Soon the work would be under the roof above the obstacle. He just wrote and sent it to him. Quickly the work will be completed without delay. After a time passed, behold the splendor of the palace that I have built, and how diligent the workmen were that I hired to build it with me. The king received the news and sent gold as soon as he heard it. He was very pleased that the palace was rising quickly. But the apostle took it and went to the poor and distributed it. He scattered it in a land that bore sixty and a hundredfold fruits. Everyone who heard it was astonished at the process, because he spent the gold and not a stone was built on the palace. Heralds ran to the king, and just as the Babylonians ran to Darius from Daniel (Dan. 6:13), for the news which they had received. Yet, the news excited the king like a sea, and more than the sea's waves he let out words and poured out anger. He roared like a lion and spat out violence like a serpent when he threatened, and he sharpened his strength against the honest man.

He came to the city and sent and called for him and Chaban. He said to Thomas: "Where is the palace that you have built? You have beautiful love for me, Chaban, for I have repaid you for making you great. For having honored you, you have insulted me through your mischief. You have seen that the gold that I gave away lavishly wandered out. It is foolish for you how unusual all this is. You bought me a servant under the name of an artist, who threw away my treasures, laid waste to my house and the palace. You are the ally in the art of cunning for the servant you bought. You threw the gold of my kingdom into the streets. Already on the way you have a contract in a secret, hidden way with one another that decided to rob me by means of architecture. It is horrifying that I gave gold and you saw it, how I was robbed while you were rejoicing, and I did not notice it."

The king said: "Where is the palace and the gold that you received? Where is it built? I will go and see it, and if there is anything missing from it, I will give it. Grant me to see him, and let my heart rejoice in his edification. I will see his houses and his chambers, whether they are finished, and whether they lie one after the other as you measured. I want to see whether the waters flow towards the palace or whether they are still far away. Maybe his water pipes are not laid and that's why they don't flow in. Did it rise completely as you drew it, or is something missing? Was your mind wrong or did everything rise after your measurements? Did some of the windows change in your measurements, or did it gradually increase in height according to the drawing? Are its walls too weak or its doors too low, or is there some other fault in the windows, beams or in its construction? Where is the gold that I gave into your hands, where did it go? To whom did you give it and where is the palace that was to be built over it? Through mine you have made yourself a righteous and benevolent person, what have you not done according to my will? To strangers you have been praised as a benefactor and as a pious one and benevolent, but not through your gold or through my gold. It was not your business to distribute mine among the poor. It only makes me uncomfortable because of the laughter, and the fact that I have been made contemptibly ridiculous saddens me more than the loss of the gold. Either show me the palace you built as you promised or refund me the gold you took to build it."

Thomas said: "Well, O king, do not be angry, calm down, I will justify myself before your majesty. The palace is built, its appearance is beautiful, and its construction is powerful. There are no artists who understand how great its value is."

The king said, "Where is it?"

Thomas replied: "It is up in heaven."

The king asked: "When will I see him now?"

Thomas replied: "In the world to come. When you get up again, you can see him in the great, infinite light."

THE PALACE THAT THE APOSTLE THOMAS BUILT

The king said, "You shall not come forward and mock me. Give me the gold, and the palace which you have built shall be yours. But if, as you claim, it was built by you in heaven above, who will lead me up by a ladder to the house of the rulers? You would first have to make a ladder and then build the palace at a height that is unknown to me. Make a ladder, and I will believe in the palace that you have built. If I see these, I believe you about what you said. Let us count the branches of this which can stand on the earth, and believe in him who is in heaven, that his buildings may be lifted up. When I see these, whose base is set up on the earth, I do not consider it to be a lie, whose structure is erected on high."

Thomas replied: "You must get yourself new wings and with them you can fly without needing a ladder."

The king said: "Such words are unnecessary. Give me back the gold and Chaban will be the owner of the palace. I do not want a palace on high without a ladder. Give to him who climbs up without the rungs of the ladder. Go, sell him, weigh the price that you received for it and bring back what you have taken, since I cannot fly into the air and climb up to see him. Where did you put the gold, the palace was not built, and how can I believe that the palace was built in heaven? When did you have wings to fly in the air? When did you build the palace on high while you were on the earth? When you ascended to heaven, tell me at what time? If you have built it on high from the earth, tell us how? Wherever it was possible to build it, it was not built, but in a distant and hidden place, in a hiding place my dwelling shall be. I bought you, a man, to build on the earth, not to build in heaven. You are a man, not a God who lives on high. Give me the gold back and go and live in the palace that you built. I didn't want the palace, why did you bother?"

Thomas replied, "O king, the gold has been distributed and it cannot really become yours again. It flew up and never returned to its owners. Don't tear yourself apart with anger that I would have worked for nothing for the same thing, I gave it to the workers so that they built the palace that I told you about. Do not be angry because the palace was built and made you poor."

THE PALACE THAT THE APOSTLE THOMAS BUILT

The king heard this again and his anger rose like smoke, and he ordered Thomas and Chaban be thrown into prison, while he thought about their cruel execution. He sent them away while he considered their scourging. They led him away, bound her, locked her up while he thought how and in what way he should kill him. Servants came and dragged him away from the royal palace and immediately took him to prison. While the king was contemplating to kill and destroy them, he did not know that the Lord was their helper. While he made up his mind to kill them, he did not yet know that he would surely worship. While he was committing murder, the life he was receiving was hidden from him. As he sharpened his sword, he became a sheep in the flock. While he contemplated death, new life was reserved for him. He thought to hold judgment tomorrow and while the fire was ready, like the Babylonians, for the despisers of the image, unknown to him that he too would worship like his colleague and bow his head like Nebuchadnezzar did (Dan. 3). While he was locked in the fold, he locked up the bridegrooms. While he was being hunted in secret, he locked the hunter in the prison. He sent them away while he pondered their torments, not knowing that the Lord had frustrated the counsel of the nations (Ps. 33:10).

Gad, his brother, heard what had happened and was shaken. He wanted to know the truth of what had happened. He learned the truth and he was depressed and saddened. He heard it and was disturbed and dismayed; He became beside himself and very distressed, and soon fell into a serious illness. But the grief over what had happened to his brother caused his death. He didn't know what to say after that. The fire of death suddenly flared up in his limbs. It was burned and consumed, like the plant that was hit by the fire. Death came in and stood on his pillow at his head and he saw him and trembled. He sent and summoned the king and recommended his possession to him. And he said to him, "My brother, I go the way of everyone, and all that I possess with my heirs will be put into your hands. The time is coming when I will go to my fathers. Protect my possessions and be a father to my sons and to me. Do not turn your attention away from the deeds of that magician, whose affair is the cause of my descent into Sheol before my time."

THE PALACE THAT THE APOSTLE THOMAS BUILT

The king replied: "Don't worry about it. I'll reassure you about him. I thought about him and his deeds all night long and made the decision to throw him alive into the fire."

While these passionate words were spoken, his soul left him; but the king left his brother's dwelling and went on his way. Then the angels descended like streams and took the soul and brought it first to the place of horror to show him. But they removed the soul from its nest like vultures, and immediately brought it to the place of fire to instill terror in it. The angels guided the soul and gradually flew, turning here and there, to show it the terrible depths. He saw the sea of flames and people in it, the stream of fire that streamed out from it and burned. He saw angels with coals falling from their wings and rolling balls of fire on the wrongdoers. He saw adulterers and adulteresses who had defiled their way of life, with a burning flame in their limbs. He also saw those who refused milk to their children, and there was fire in their breasts and in them the women also hung. She saw Abraham and Lazarus on the right and the rich man and his fellow party members on the left. She saw the sinners being martyred in the darkness in terrible judgments of mighty fire in a terrible way. After she had now been sufficiently shaken and wandered around and had seen all the damned, the merciful ones supported him, and he succeeded and came to the place of life. He turned away from the darkness and swung up to the place full of light, with the guardian angels holding her hands and guiding her. He came to the palace that the apostles had built and saw its splendor. He was amazed and astonished when she saw it. He was beside himself with the palace of light that had created its likeness, with its great splendor and with its immense beauty. He saw it like the old palace of the sun standing on high and its light flaming, with rays of brilliance surrounding it on all sides. A fragrance arose from him that surpassed the balsamic scents. She also recovered from the torture into which he had fallen. He saw his rooms and apartments and the splendor of it all. He bowed down and worshiped the angels and said to them: "If I have found favor before you, I ask you, let me recover a little from my torments here and stay in the shade of the palace for a little while, that I may recover here, having been put into great fear."

The angels answered the soul's request: "It is impossible, for it has a master who bought it and for whom it is kept. The palace belongs to your brother, but he doesn't know it. Thomas built it with the gold he received from him. Your Hebrew built this palace with your brother's property, and it is impossible for anyone to enter it without it. He took his keys after he had locked it, and if he does not open it, no one can open it, enter into it, or stay in it. Ask your brother to sell it to you, whom he does not know. Bring the keys and come, enter, stay there, nothing will stop you."

He answered: "I will now go at once and not delay, lest he receive knowledge from him and then not sell it. Dismiss me, I want to go and buy the palace from him and then come back. It's my brother who owns it and he sells it to me who he doesn't know."

The angels said, "No one goes from here to there, unless the day of judgment is at hand, to the people and tribes, but go and say to the king: 'That Hebrew whom he has bound, behold you shall not torment, lest the palace become a part of another.' Innumerably his (Thomas) rule is greater than yours and his does not fade or change like yours. A throne surrounded with glory is reserved for him here, on which he will sit, and he will judge the tribes with his companions in the last days. Do not offend the Holy One who rules over all; for if you sin against him, you will pay the debts that you have committed. Go, show the king the way in which he should go, that he may forsake the error of idolatry in which he walks. Tell him what kind of palace Thomas has built for him and where, if he wishes, his possessions are located."

The angels released the soul to go to their Geuossen (the body) with the words: "Make sure you don't forget anything of what you have seen."

While the body was wrapped, with bandages or in a cloth, so that it was carried out and buried, the soul returned in the morning to the nest from which it had flown back. The dead man returned to life and assumed movements and feelings. The dead man awoke after the sleep of death had left him. The man who was lost in sleep moved, opened his eyes and looked at the crowd. As soon as he spoke, the mute man began so that his friends would please him. He said: "Loosen my hands and feet which you have bound to me, so that I am free."

THE PALACE THAT THE APOSTLE THOMAS BUILT

But his friends received him like a prisoner returning to his place. "Call the king to me quickly; I have a request for him. I was asked to make a message to him. Make him come soon. Tell him your brother has arrived and has come from a friend, tell him a letter from there that he wants to show you. Tell him the king, the lord of the place, sent him a letter. Come, read and see what is written in it and give an answer. Tell him that he will come and hear news that will delight him. What he thought was lost I have found; he shouldn't worry any more.

The new message, full of life, reached the king: "Your brother, O king, has previously revived and sent for you. After he was wrapped and his hands were bound and his feet bound, he rose from the bed and now sits on it, waiting for you. Cries of lamentation were uttered like the sound of thunder; and like streams the tears flowed from pupils. But while the women raised lamentations like drunken ones and everyone was in a mood of mourning as if he were being buried, and while men and women, old and young wept for him and neither a stranger nor a local suspected it, his limbs moved and he opened his eyes and saw the crowd. Your Highness was the first thing he asked for as soon as he spoke. 'Call to me', said he, 'the king, to come. I have a request for him. Let him speak immediately, I long to see him. I came today from a guest friend like a businessman. I have something to tell him, he should come quickly.'

The king heard these words and trembled. He left and quickly hurried out of his palace. He came to his brother and saw him with astonishment and horror. But because he was astonished, he did not believe it, not even after he had seen him. He wept and was both very happy and confused. He looked at him to see if he could tell his brother about the palace that the apostle Thomas built in India. He cried and was of divided opinion about the truth of the fact. The king said, "Tell us what you have seen. What are the dead like there, and who do they resemble? Do they know each other there or not? Is the consciousness preserved there, or has it ceased from anything? Does it exist there and hope to come to the resurrection? Does it expect to come to the resurrection or is it gone? Furthermore, are high and low, small and great found, or are they one and not differentiated in their position? Is the king honored, the rich respected and the poor despised, or are they not known? Does one person there speak to another about what he has done, or is the thread of silence stretched out over everyone?"

Gad said to him, "Do not ask my brother what you have said. For there is no time to tell you what I have seen. If it is possible, I will ask you to let me have something. I will pay you the price for it and buy it from you like a stranger. What I ask you do not know, but I know it. The price leaves it to me like a stranger."

The king replied: "Once I know what you want, take as much as you want, without price. I will give you half of my kingdom if you ask me for it. And all the more as I see you alive, take the crown on my head. I really don't need anything besides you, just tell me what you want and I'll grant it to you."

Gad replied: "You promised not to deny me. Give me the palace that the apostle Thomas built for you. I only ask you for this, do not refuse it to me. This is what I ask of you, O king, of everything you own. Give this to me and now take everything I own. And while I pay you well the value, do not refuse me it. Take my palaces with my possessions. But I now receive it as my possession. Hereupon I write to you everything that I own, along with my buildings, my possessions and my pure inheritances."

The king said, "If what you said is true, then give to you all that I have, and leave the palace to its lord. Lord, the man who built it is alive, and he does not lie. Tell this to him, and he will certainly build one for you. The building artist is there, who is happy to be able to build. There are also workers there. Give him gold and he will build one for you, just as he built one for me. But if I have a palace in heaven and you have seen it, I will not take the whole world and give it to you. If he built a palace among the angels, as you said, I would not exchange a room with him for the whole world. As soon as I found out that I have a palace beyond death, how will I give my great jewelry to someone else? Don't push me any further if I don't give in to this thing. Sea and land are not considered to me like his shadow. Let us go and see if the apostle who built it is still alive, and let us ask him to forgive us our sins against him. Come, brother, let us bring him out of prison into the light. For India has been in darkness since we enclosed him. Come, my brother, let us go and bring out the light that was hidden from us, so that the world, which is full of hatred and has been robbed of its idols, may be filled by the light. Come, my brother, let us go, let us lead out of the prison the prisoner who heals the sick and casts out demons from humanity. Come, my brother, let us go and implore the good one for mercy, by whose prayers the Lord pardons and forgives us. Come, my brother, let us go to the Holy One against whom we have sinned, who, although he had committed no offense against us, is shut up and imprisoned. Come, my brother, let us go to the Builder of all souls, who is a Comforter and Physician of all sinners."

The king and his brother arose to go to the prison. They raised their voices and said to the inhabitant of the house: "Servant of the Lord, come, get out of the prison now! Through the knowledge of the truth, we ask you, attend to the words. We have now come to free you and loosen your bonds. Free us, Lord, from that yoke of image worship!"

The apostle went to the prison with great pomp, the king and his brother on his side and on his left. They kissed and hugged and asked him to forgive their sins like his Lord. They recited to him the words of the one who came on the way from Cush: "Behold, there is water, which prevents us from being baptized anymore."

The apostle stood over the water and made the sign of the cross over it the water, then called the king and his brother with him and baptized them- in the name of the Father and of the Son and of the Spirit he baptized them. But all the thorns of their sins remained in the water. Blessed be he who sent the apostle Thomas to the land of India to teach and baptize and to turn blacks into whites. Blessed be he who gave his church strength and triumph in his name; and caused constant praise to arise for him from every mouth, which gave victory to the apostle Thomas. God be praised at all times. Amen, amen!

The poem about the palace that the Apostle Thomas commanded is complete.

The Scriptorium Project is the work of a small group of lay people of various apostolic churches who are interested in the preservation, transmission, and translation of the works of the early and medieval church. Our efforts are to make the works of the church fathers accessible to anyone who might have an interest in Christian antiquities and the theological, philosophical, and moral writings that have become the bedrock of Western Civilization.

To-date, our releases have pulled from the Greek, Syriac, Georgian, Latin, Celtic, Ethiopian, and Coptic traditions of Christianity, and have been pulled from sundry local traditions and languages.

Other Selections from the Syriac Church Series:

Writings by St. Cyprian of Antioch (Jan. 2009)

Laws or Plans by Isaiah of Syria (Dec. 2009)

The Palace that the Apostle Thomas Built in India by St. Jacob of Serug (Feb. 2010)

The Virtuous Life by St. Isaac of Nineveh (July 2010)

History of the Conversion of the Georgian to Christianity by Marcarius III of Antioch (Aug. 2010)

Four Works by St. Isaac of Nineveh (Oct. 2012)

Life of St. Mary the Harlot by St. Ephrem the Syrian (May 2014)

Fragments by St. Ephraim of Antioch (Mar. 2018)

The Syriac Menologium and Martyrology (Nov 2022)

The Syriac Life of John the Baptist by Serapion the Presbyter (June 2023)

www.ingramcontent.com/pod-product-compliance
Lightning Source LLC
LaVergne TN
LVHW051923060526
838201LV00060B/4162